Mixed Bag
A Travelogue in Four Forms

William Scott Galasso

GALWIN PRESS

Mixed Bag: A Travelogue in Four Forms
Published by GALWIN PRESS
LAGUNA WOODS, CALIFORNIA

Copyright ©2018 WILLIAM SCOTT GALASSO.
All rights reserved.

No part of this book may be reproduced in any form or by any mechanical means, including information storage and retrieval systems without permission in writing from the publisher/author, except by a reviewer who may quote passages in a review.

All images, logos, quotes, and trademarks included in this book are subject to use according to trademark and copyright laws of the United States of America.

Library of Congress Control Number: 2018911757
GALASSO, WILLIAM SCOTT, Author
MIXED BAG
WILLIAM SCOTT GALASSO

ISBN: **978-1-7327527-0-2**

POETRY / Subjects & Themes / Places
POETRY / Haiku

Cover design by Deanna Estes, Lotus Design

QUANTITY PURCHASES: Schools, companies, professional groups, clubs, and other organizations may qualify for special terms when ordering quantities of this title. For information, email galwinpress@yahoo.com.

All rights reserved by WILLIAM SCOTT GALASSO
and GALWIN PRESS.

This book is printed in the United States of America.

To Vicki, wife, friend and partner on this
thirty-year journey, love and gratitude

Foreword

Mixed Bag: A Travelogue in Four Forms, is the first in a legacy series of poems written over a period of fifty years. The work has been culled from fourteen previous books and includes added new material written over the last three years. Several of these pieces have been published in journals and anthologies but have not yet appeared in previous books.

I have used four forms of poems in this collection. These forms consist of short poems in free verse mode, plus haiku sequences, haibun and tanka which are Japanese style verses. They are illustrations of my own contemporary journeys and yet in some ways they contain an echo of classical Japanese journeys made by writers like Matsuo Basho, the author of *Narrow Road to the Interior* for example.

While classic Japanese poets such as Buson, Basho, Shiki and Issa wrote from a cultural perspective based on the largely agrarian environment, my own work celebrates my own contemporary, more urban culture.

I have chosen to assemble each section in a particular way, which is to intersperse haibun and haiku sequences by region. Short poem sections and tanka are given their own space in order to speak in their own voice to address specific subject matter. In effect, my purpose was to give the effect of a travelogue "a breathing in of haibun and the sequences," "a breathing out" of short poems and tanka". I chose this route because all of these poems in their way essentially speak to a "poetry of place".

The Forms

Tanka

Tanka poems are a traditional Japanese style of poetry that will follow a set pattern of syllables in a 5-7-5-7-7 format. In other words, there are five syllables in the first and third lines and seven syllables in lines two, four, and five.

Contemporary Tanka in English adheres generally to the five-line format, but the syllable count, though usually under 32 is not uniformly 5-7-5-7-7.

Haibun

The term "*haibun*" was first used by the 17th-century Japanese poet Matsuo Basho in 1690. Bashō was a prominent early writer of *haibun*, then a new genre combining classical prototypes, Chinese prose genres and vernacular subject matter and language. He wrote some *haibun* as travel accounts during his various journeys, the most famous of which is Oku no Hosomichi (*Narrow Road to the Interior*).

Traditional *haibun* typically took the form of a short description of a place, person or object, or a diary of a journey or other series of events in the poet's life.

In English

Haibun is no longer confined to Japan, and has established itself as a worldwide genre in literature which has gained momentum in recent years.

The first contest for English language *haibun* took place in 1996, organized by poet and editor Michael Dylan Welch, and judged by Tom Lynch and Cor van den Heuvel. Jim Kacian and Bruce Ross edited the inaugural number of the annual anthology *Contemporary Haibun* in 2003 and sponsored the parallel creation in 2005 of *Contemporary Haibun Online*.

Characteristics

A *haibun* may record a scene, or a special moment, in a highly descriptive and objective manner or may occupy a wholly fictional or dream-like space. The accompanying haiku may have a direct or subtle relationship with the prose and encompass or hint at the gist of what is recorded in the prose sections.

Several distinct schools of English *haibun* have been described, including *Reportage narrative mode* such as Robert Wilson's *Vietnam Ruminations*, *Haibunic prose*, and the *Templum effect*.

Contemporary practice of *haibun* composition in English is continually evolving.

My note: (Counting syllables is not as important, due to differences between English speaking and Japanese traditional language and cultural differences). Generally, a *haibun* consists of one or more paragraphs of prose written in a concise, imagistic *haikai* style, and one or more haiku. However, there may be considerable variation of form, as described by editor and practitioner Jeffrey Woodward.

Modern English

NORTHEAST HAIBUN

Card Flipping Boys of Summer

This was a ritual practiced by boys every spring and summer since the last century was young. Its variations were innumerable. In Long Island, NY where I grew up you could play "colors", "teams", or "positions." Players would take turns flipping cards face-up, the winner "trumping" the loser's card. For example, if someone threw down a "Yankee" card and the next player threw another "Yankee" card, the latter would "win the pot" having trumped the former. The same principle held for each variation and the "dealer" called the game.

This was a boy's Las Vegas; everyone had
a system and the games were earnestly
played on long summer days. On occasion
the pot would grow quite large and as the
stakes increased the tension grew.

flipping baseball cards,
turning ever more slowly
as the pot grows

Hailing the Policeman

This haibun was inspired by an article, which appeared throughout the country and was reported by a local patrolman in Eastern Pennsylvania. It seems that the officer was driving down the road and had to hit the breaks as a duck flew at him. Not wanting to harm the creature he backed up and started to go around the duck. However, the duck would have none of it, she flapped her wings, quacked vociferously and flew up at the car. Sensing something odd, the officer got out of his car and followed the duck to one side of the road. Again, it quacked, flapped its wings and waddled towards a storm drain. The officer bent down to find that nearly a dozen ducklings were frantically trying to keep from being carried down into a pipe beneath the storm drain.

He lifted the grate and one by one plucked
the ducklings out of danger, depositing
each beside their mother. Mother duck and
her brood now reunited trundled to the
opposite side of the road and crossed into a
gently moving stream.

        caught in a storm drain-
        the ducklings' mother
        hails a policeman

Park Visit

Years ago, I lived in the town of Roslyn Harbor, N.Y. and frequently rode my bike along the North Shore of Long Island. One of the places I enjoyed visiting was a smallish park in the nearby town of Sea Cliff. The park was situated on a bluff overlooking Long Island Sound with a view north of the Connecticut Coast. The park, though not large, had its share of flora and fauna, including oak, maple, birch, pine and one or two blue spruce. The variety of birds included crows, blue jays, red-winged blackbirds, sparrows, robins (in spring), and being by the sound, gulls. During migrations in spring and fall, there were geese and mallards as well. The park also had a few animals typical of woodland areas, among them squirrels, chipmunks, the occasional raccoon usually seen at dusk, and of course, neighborhood dogs and cats. It was a quiet place enjoyed by the locals.

One autumn day, I happened to be musing at the passing clouds when I heard the sound of a child at play; leaves were falling and one had brushed his face. It was then I noticed that the child was blind, past the stage of being a toddler, but still very young. I watched as he sniffed the air declaring "salt." His mother explained that was the smell of the sea, which here became the Sound. "It's like a big bath tub, with one side open," she explained. The boy ran around the park (his Mother always within arms-length), enjoying all its textures and every time he touched something his mother would say that's a "bench," or this is "iron" as she lifted him up and as he touched the rough bark she said "tree." The little boy would repeat every word.

Soon, a friendly little neighborhood cat came by and the mother sat the boy down and called "kitty, kitty." The little cat came to snake itself around their feet as cat's do. She said "Now honey, I want you to touch this cat at your feet—but be very gentle, just brush his fur like this and taking his hand had him pet the cat. "She's so soft." "Yes". The contented cat made a purring sound.

The little boys face lit up, "Is that the cat?" he asked. "Yes, dear." "She sounds Happy—I like that sound." "Yes, it's very sweet," replied his mother. I sat quietly. I didn't want to intrude though I heard every word, I smiled, felt my eyes begin to fill, but not for pity; "love" was a word he already knew.

        blind child's visit--
       for everything touched
        a gift of new words

Paper Route 1960

As an eight-year old I took a summer job as a newspaper delivery boy. I'd grab an armful of papers, put them in the basket of my Schwinn, and deliver newspapers to several neighborhoods near my house on Long Island. It was a way to earn a little money, while enjoying fine summer weather.

        daybreak
       the slow glide
      of seven swans

On my route lived an elderly lady, who liked the papers delivered to her in person, no toss to the driveway for her. Of course, I didn't know what to expect that first time I went to her house. The widow's housekeeper let me in and offered me cookies and milk. The house had been the summer get-away home originally and had an elegant yet worn feel to it. Over time, I learned that Mrs. B had lived in the house for over fifty years. Her husband had been a veteran of the Civil War and "nearly twenty years older than her when they married," but he was handsome and kind she assured me.

    grandma's house—
   morning sun alights on
   objects of another time

Except for Sundays when a man came to drive her to church, the routine was pretty much the same. I'd sit on the chair near Mrs. B., (happily munching on cookies with milk or lemonade), while she would take a few minutes and tell me a little about her life. One day she told me her son had been one of Roosevelt's Rough Riders and had died during the charge up San Juan Hill. Her eyes moistened as she showed me his picture.

        forever young
      the apple that fell
       near the tree

Another time, she spoke of her daughter,
who had married and moved all the way to
Chicago. She smiled as she told me about
her grand-daughters one a dancer,
another a teacher.

      her children's children
       so many smiles
        for grandma

After a while she'd say "OK, young man
scoot, you've got a job to do." As I got up
to leave, she'd press a quarter in my hand.

       summer cycling--
    under trees the shift
     of sun and shade

I had the paper route for a few summers,
in time she became sort of a surrogate
Grandma.

After school when the weather was good, I'd occasionally visit just to say Hi, (besides the cookies were always a treat). I began to notice though, how thin she became, the skin on her hands like paper lace. Her frail body almost disappearing beneath the hand knit shawl she wore. She had turned one hundred.

    birthday candles
she musters her strength
to blow them all out

One day a nurse opened the door, she's ill
I was told. Next day, Mary, the
housekeeper, said that Mrs. B. had
passed in her sleep. Then Mary pressed
into my hands an envelope with Mrs. B's
scrawl, in it was a $10.00 bill, a veritable
fortune and a U.S. Eagle button.

        Winter solstice
    the last of the leaves
          descending

EVENT SEQUENCES

September 11, 2001
(dedicated with respect to the victims
and to those who died that others might
live)

at the sound
of collapsing towers,
pigeons take flight

day becomes night
in a gloaming of smoke,
beepers under rubble

watching a jet pass
overhead, another
deep breath taken

our cat, unable
to read the news
sleeps soundly

where twin towers stood,
the emptiness of sky
...and missing persons

**AFTER SANDY
(ELEGY FOR PAUMANOK+)**

the sea recalls
not only names
written in sand
but the dunes
which in youth
hid our lovemaking

+ the big fish, Native American
term for Long Island, NY

SEQUENCES OF PLACE
U.S. (NORTHEAST)

New York/Pennsylvania

boardwalk, Jones Beach
sea salt and cigar smoke
marinate the air

Matinecock grave—
between two boulders
new leaves on the old oak

Broadway at dusk
rain and neon glaze
the city's streets

fireflies
in the wheat field
...Gettysburg

9/11/2001

Fort Sumter
seven American flags
flying at half-mast

**SEQUENCES OF PLACE
U.S. (SOUTHEAST)**

SOJOURN SOUTH
(Georgia, South Carolina)

Tybee Island,
the spartina swaying
beneath egret wings,

Andersonville—
under Georgia's red earth
so many unknowns

squall in Savannah
cool rain numbing
mosquito bites

Sunday morning
Charleston, the smell
of hot biscuits

palmetto cockade,
old secesh symbol now
a tourist souvenir

Boone Plantation—
at the riverside boat dock
thousands of oyster shells

smashed mini balls
was it only dirt or flesh
and bone they found

moonlight on cabins
of the old slave street
low moan of wind

FLORIDA SEQUENCE I

rice field ritual
the egrets elaborate dance
mating time again

driving to Key West
miles of ocean spitting salt
four lanes of concrete

husky Seminole
scratching the gator's belly
suddenly...it sleeps

Everglade boating
mosquitoes and snakes
bites and BITES

blond wearing a tan
her tiny suit says "Guess"
...I don't have to

standing on one leg
the pink flamingo in mud
goose-like honks

sand between toes
sun drying sea from my skin
tomorrow...snow boots

FLORIDA SEQUENCE II

twenty-three hawks
wheeling and circling
wings crowd the sky

swamp in winter
bare trees, empty nest
the gators sleep

morning stillness
inland waterway
birthing hibiscus

tropical storm
raining the gray
into blue seas

bisecting water
the boats wake
a spreading V

too long at sea
sailors mistake manatees
for mermaids

Indian River...
pink flamingoes on
tailored lawns

campground full
moonbeams bathe
the launchpad

HAIBUN-NORTHWEST

THE MAN WHO LOVES HUMMINGBIRDS

I have always enjoyed birds, of all varieties. As a child, I was fascinated by flight and imagined the wonderful views the birds must have as they traversed the sky. There were the native species; blue jays, red-winged blackbirds, cardinals, crows whose antics and "smokers cough" voices amused me. There was also the mournful cry of gulls and a myriad of number shore birds; including terns, sandpipers as I lived a few miles from the sea. The hardy ducks and mallards impressed me as well, as they swam in the frigid ponds, in the dead of winter. In addition, the migrations of geese signaled the turn of seasons and spring was ushered in when the robins returned. At all times, I enjoyed hearing their many and varied songs.

        chevrons in the sky
        the geese honk out
          their cadence

I did not have much experience of hummingbirds though until I moved to the Pacific Northwest. Here, they're more common, especially the Rufous Hummingbird and Anna's Hummingbird. We have some plants in our garden that attract them, as well as a hummingbird feeder or two, which provides the sugar water they like, an alternative to nectar. We also have Delphinium and Honeysuckle, which they enjoy.

           descending
         summer breeze
        the hummingbird
        sits on Lucifer*

    * a varietal of Crocosmia

But we are far outdone in our love for them by the MAN WHO LOVES HUMMINGBIRDS. An Oregonian, his entire Garden is designed to lure these fragile but wondrous birds to his domain. He has every plant and shrub, known to attract them; Thimbleberry, Red-Flowering Current, Western Columbine, Delphinium, Penstemon serrrulatus, red gooseberry, salmonberry, huckleberry. He has willow, cascara, bitter cherry and crabapple trees. His garden in full, a hummingbird paradise and from almost every tree a feeder is hung, lest the nectar fall short.

        cornucopia
        garden scents shift
        with the west wind

Recently, an ornithologist proclaimed that the garden contained nearly two hundred hummingbirds.

The Man Who Loves Hummingbirds smiled,
stood in the midst of his garden, with eyes
closed and arms outstretched.
Hummingbirds flew close by, stopped and
hovered around him, then returned to the
frenetic pace of their flight.

        flash and dart
        of color, the air
        alive with sound

EDMONDS—A HAIBUN IN FOUR PARTS

Morning

Glow in the East, night rises, departs. The greater orb, spills its light, rays razor through branches of cedar, spruce, hemlock and oak. Birds lift their voices in a praise song of chirps and trills, as gulls and crows not contending, add their screech and cackle. Shadows lengthen, slowly to dissipate, a sea breeze rich in salt, shivers the leaves of Japanese maples and the garden flowers bend and stretch. Morning glories open, red and yellow roses, purple lavender gift color and scent. Blue stars, saxifrage and sedum speckle the brown of earth while green ferns fill in the dappled sun and shade.

daybreak...
here a chickadee,
there a warbler

Noon

Wide awake, no place to hide. Fruit ripens
on the trees; Anjou pears, plums, Red
delicious apples and figs. Near Puget
Sound the whistles of trains cleave the air,
contending with the shush of passing cars
or the occasional clunk of trucks. But on
the Sound, Commerce too hustles by:
trawlers, freighters, tugs and barges ply
the sea, each half hour the ferries
crisscross from mainland to island. Feet in
the sand where tides erase names, baring
witness to the silent stalk of Blue Herons
and the noisy competition of gulls. To each
his own fish. To the west, Olympic
Mountains pierce clouds, playing truth or
dare with those who would seek their
wisdom, attempt their peaks.

more than words
for purple mountains majesty
straight-ahead, due west

Evening

In the evening, we sit on our deck, in the bowl that hugs our house. There we sip wine, as the day runs its course, our reward for the labor we do. We hear the distant laughter of the children in playgrounds, the occasional siren, maybe a barking dog. Yet, for the most part the sounds are soothing and time seems held in abeyance. We watch the pleasure boats glide by, sails slipping into silhouette. In summer, cruise ships pass, plying the tourists North to Alaska or South to Seattle. We wish them joy in their journey, content to be their audience. Dancing diamonds of silver, slowly migrate to gold in Puget Sound, the sky acquiring fire from the setting sun; Olympic mountains to the West, rise ridge on ridge, mist gathering in the valleys. The red suns drops like a coin in a slot, the clouds both purple and pink.

>   a sailor's delight sky
>   first stars pierce the pale
>   yet deepening blue

Night

Afterglow gives way to indigo. One by one, as if responding to the call of stars, the town spreads its own Milky Way of light, renders the darkling coastline visible. A sliver of cirrus bisects the moon like a ghostly finger fading, the quiet deepens until it becomes just the moth on the window, looking in. Some nights we love, some nights we dream, others pass with the turn of the page. She sleeps, untroubled, her breathing a whisper, our little dog lies beside her and snores.

The last ferry, lit up like a birthday cake,
heads to Kingston. I fill my lungs by the
window. I am where I began in a home by
the sea.

so much depends upon
the smell of salt and
a star to steer by

**SEQUENCES OF PLACE
U.S. - (NORTHWEST)**

THE DAY AFTER CHRISTMAS

silent night
flake upon flake
the deepening snow

ice
shape shifting into
twigs and branches

mantled in white
evergreen branches
kow tow to roots

pale sun...still rye grass...fog

hot coffee,
busy shovels scratching,
scraping

near the fire
lips and loins unite
against the freeze

all night long
in the darkness
falling trees

sparrows
yesterday's garage
today's sanctuary

morning...rain, just rain

WINTER STORM

snowflakes...
so many millions
none alike

cabin fever
the snow falls
and falls
.....and falls

bending
under the whiteness
evergreens

garage bound
sparrow, trapped
or hiding out

morning
small ponds frozen
on the windowsill

in the snow
deer tracks...
cougar tracks

horizontal crawl
clouds and
chimney smoke

a patch of blue
shadows appear
the icicles drip

PORTLAND SEQUENCE

graveyard of ships
where river and sea collide
cold bones in the deep

roundball ritual
Rose City to Rip City
Blazermania

my life in letters
koi fanning water
small fish, big pond

movie prop thicket
roses steal the scenery
people scuttled out

composing haiku
rock garden perfection
teaching humility

**STP (Seattle To Portland)
Bicycle Ride**

Pre-dawn, full moon
only wheels turning
and lark song

over the lake, sunrise
fog lifts over cool water,
scent of roses

too fast around the turn
rider sprawls on pavement,
saved by his helmet

Near Puyallup,
chug of heavy breathing
on the uphill climb

rest stop, Centralia
surveying tomorrow's map
half-way home

Oregon crossing
at Longview, wind riffles hair
on the downhill run

Mt. St. Helen's stop
all eyes fixate on it,
cool water on the neck

St. John's bridge,
music, cold beer waiting
finish line, goose bumps

The Rose Garden (Portland, OR)

The deaf actress
drinking sight and scent
signs beautiful

SEAVIEW SEQUENCE

after lovemaking
the smile adorning her face
becoming my own

waves and blowing sand
plovers at water's edge
racing clouds... converge

at vanishing point
sandpiper's braving wind
between land and sea

wandering tattler
crying six plaintive notes
...gossiping solo

sand dune graffiti
beer bottles and condoms
teenage habitat

filling my footsteps
a million sun-caught grains
sand washed by waves

SEATTLE and environs

Dimitriou's Jazz Alley

in a jazz club
that a decade ago
would be wreathed in
cirrus clouds of blue
Pinetop Perkins shaves
piano keys with hands
a hundred years old

floating over
Puget Sound, notes from
the jazzman's clarinet

road to Emerald City
paved with yellow leaves
the passing cars toss

lights glide
across Puget Sound
ferry through the fog

Snoqualmie Falls
transformed the snow,
in full voice roars

over Mt. Rainier
lenticular clouds,
I file a memory

lights glide
across Puget Sound
ferry through the fog

WASHINGTON STATE/HAWAII HAIBUN

Puget Sound/Kauai

three weeks running a drone of gray days;
fog, haze in the morning, showers strafe
streets scratched by fallen leaves and at
night, the rhythmic percussion of water
slapping each roof in slow migration.

gloom and doom
in print, on the radio
no respite

Next day, a metallic scent of snow, a
freeze that troubles even the marrow, a
sparrow stiff, hard beside the window, our
dog sniffs, shivers, runs inside, hides in her
blanket, needing a week of escape, we
book our flight

refugees huddled
in a flying cattle car
yesteryear's steerage

over the islands lush and green, palm trees
taro fields, white sand beaches, jackets
shed like autumn leaves, a scent of
flowers, a gift of leis, the sound of slack
key guitars, smiles warm as toast

Na Pali coast
Spinner dolphins act out,
children too

for days, we swim in blue and green seas
and taste the tropics in tall glasses sweet
with mango or tart with pineapple or
coconut shave ice cool on the tongue, and
refreshed find the time for a love matinee

Poipu Beach
these Birds-of-Paradise
how aptly named this day

A day before leaving for the journey home
liquid sunshine, drenches the monkey tree
pours and pours until pools the colors of
rust form, rivers of red running the streets,
until a reprieve of a cloud break shows a
rainbow bridge in the valley

a rooster proclaims
that morning has broken,
then struts among the hens

KAUAI SEQUENCE

bursting under stars
fireworks at Poipu Beach
ring the New Year in

the voyaging whales
swimming off the Na Pali coast
waving tails...goodbye

tunnel of the trees
Eucalyptus Ave.
cycling Koloa

sea sings to Pele
moonlight at Lumahai
I, the lone witness

Since ancient time
harvesting taro route
Hanalei Valley

Waimea Canyon
passion flower offering
the gift accepted

U.S.- WEST COAST/SOUTHWEST SEQUENCES

SANTA BARBARA: RAIN SEQUENCE

California rain
the long drought ending
drop by drop

sun shower over
barefoot in wet grass
a woman sings

a bell tolling
the old mission sways
dancing in puddles

tracking a boat
the rainbow shackles
a sailor's gaze

a water wound
shaking her paw dry
the puzzled cat

train whistle
tires splashing rain
gulls squawking

in the drought year
"Brown is beautiful"
proclaims a sign

STEARN'S WHARF: SANTA BARBARA

chased by breakers,
sandpipers playing
red light, green light

thrice caressed
by sun, sea breeze
my woman's hands

by the fish market
looking for handouts
insatiable gulls

wings astride waves
the lone pelican
flying towards sunset

clouds inflamed
by dying sun
her silhouette

in the darkness
under stars
sea lion's bark

MORNING OF THE QUAKE SEQUENCE

our wide-eyed cat
on her sleeping blanket
the snoring dog

he dreams of falling
and rises before dawn
to quaking earth

no word, no power
sinister silence
finally a phone rings

a lump in her throat
hearing her mother's voice
tears...then her mother's smile

not minding the fog
we walk, hands clasped
not a word, a hug

above our heads
wind in the willows
below, who knows

California/South Dakota

renewal of faith
...the swallows return
to Capistrano

Pacific wren
the forest
finds its voice

Mid-day heat--
hawks above the Rosebud River
circling the dead

MIXED BAG SEQUENCES

TERMINAL

diagnosis confirmed,
down her cheek
slow glide of tears

nothing to say
only my hands and arms
can speak

sunrise answers,
sunset
begs a question

saying "I love you,"
often, no time
for holding back

Yes! Laugh!
loud and long
shake down these walls

one less voice
to hear, to sing
silence grows

the word
after every thought
"last"

another meeting
perhaps
...across the river

VIGIL

indigo sky
crescent moon
labored breathing

croaking frogs
startle the night
falling rain

silence...crickets
lights on, silence
off again crickets

3 A.M.
she passes on
suddenly, the wind

red eyes
softly spoken words
white orchids

her voice
in my tired mind
whispering…sleep

DRUM CIRCLE

hands on skins
warming
to the tempo

hair flying
a soloist lathers
the crowd
handclaps

eyes close
but inside...
a smile opens

in between
the big Bam BOOM
stunning silence

IN THE BEGINNING...

her dance
tightening
my jeans

snapping the wishbone
long stem, short stem...
no matter, same wish

removing her blouse
she asks what I'd like
for my birthday

as our lips meet...
me in her eyes,
she in mine

hardening
on my tongue
her nipples

her orgasm
shivers me
into mine

after...
even our breathing
slows in tune

with her eyes, asking
where I'm going
without her

THE RIFT

sharing silence
once
we had laughter

alone
all day watching
the spider spin

October
leaves fall,
like stars
and wishes

hotel bed
in your place
naked sheets

so much colder
this year, than last
...isn't it?

cease fire
still the woodpile
grows

if a word could heal,
I'd speak it.

that smile
a rare radiance
more wine?

our hands touch,
maybe
our hearts can follow.

INTERLUDE

with my eyes,
I paint
your canvas

your nakedness
more radiant
than the fire

touches me

like bow
and fiddle
we play
each other

Yes,
she does taste
finger-licking good

you rise, like the moon
I shoot, like stars
together, we blaze

in the room, two days
only the TV
left untouched

EROS SEQUENCE

removing
our bathing suits
soft caress of wind

lips and fingers
the warmth in me
moves north

midsummer night—
my toes, your heals
molding sand

peeping tom
at our window...I reach
for the Cat snacks

on my cheek
the deep red stamp
of her lipstick

coming home late,
as I approach the bed
one eye opens

LATER...

opening our wedding
album, a ray of sunshine
and motes of dust

her warmth,
still in the blankets
wrapped around me

holding her close
...at least her scent in the
perfumed pillow

at sea, under stars--
renewing our wedding vows
with a timeless kiss

riding
water bed waves
the bored cat

SHORT POEMS

SYMBIOSIS NATURUM

Escape your ego, break the chains of self
that bind you from universal consciousness.
Can you taste the salt air, do you hear the
grass grow? Do not stand and look at the
tree, be its leaves. Become the ocean roar,
fling yourself upon the sands—
become the sun, illuminate, reflect, burn.
Transcend space, make all space here and
all time, Now.

REQUIEM FOR A WHALE

What "hunter" kills with bullets
The friend who comes to call,
Who sounds her greeting joyfully
to find her faith betrayed.
She came to swim beside you
felt a harpoon's bite instead
no chanted prayer can amend
that fate, still the keening of that death.
In culture's name, slaughter begins, who
now will bar that door? There is blood in
the water, where there once was a song.

THE TEA DRINKER

Your fingers frame the cup
delicately as if in prayer.
You draw the contents to
your lips in ritual ceremony
though you're far out of site
from Mount Fuji. There is
gentleness and grace in all
of your movements as if
you held in your hands
a sparrow's beating heart.

LAKE WASHINGTON

Deep green
park grass, trees
the lake channeling waves,
the geese above the waves
the high mountains above the geese
the sun behind the clouds, stars
unseen as yet, soon
to become one
earth and sky
body and
soul

EQUILIBRIUM

My heart is not butter soft
timid in the heat of passion
and prone to melting in strife.
It is not bound with barbed wire,
where with every breath it bleeds.
Nor is it inured against injuries
real or imagined in a thousand
years of rain. It is a muscle,
a beating clock, just as strong
as it needs to be.

FLEETING

My words are wind.
I sent them out
as gifts, as flowers.
No one watered them
they withered and died,
maybe silence is best.

UNFINISHED BUSINESS

The blank stare
of a page says "fill me,"
a challenge I try to meet.
Images float by,
flotsam and jetsam,
the roof brain chatters noisily,
scribbled notes, cross outs
and curses, a futile tear
a fear of impotence
and damned desolation.

FULL TIME

I am the commodity,
I sell each day
in the marketplace.
Strangers ask ...
what have you done,
who have you been?
They peruse my papers
give me their cards,
smile and say we'll call.

STORM ON THE CUSP OF AUTUMN

Under threat of a thunderhead
whitecaps rake the lakefront sand.
Sensing change in the tremulous
wind, an osprey rises languorously
stretching wings, a turtle ventures
forth his cautious head then retreats
inside his shell, the beaver heads
homeward towards his wood
and wattle den, only I am caught
unaware running in the rain.

GIVING THANKS

In the time
when apples ripen,
when leaves wear
brazen scarlet or
mimic fool's gold
and pumpkins make
faces at passers-by,
I walk at sunset in air
that smells of snow,
just to fill my lungs
an ocean deep and breathe,
just breathe

ALL THIS...

is given to me;
cricket chirp in the meadow
bird trill flitting from tree to tree
soft shuffle of deer near a salt lick
the flow of stream into river
river into sea, where I another
sleek creature immerse myself
in a silent baptism of peace.

TRANSMIGRATION

The sun plays hide and seek
as clouds pass, leaves fall
snow dissolves in the froth
of waves. Rain cracks granite,
mountains slip into mountain streams;
even stars die and our bodies
become soil, wombs to shelter
future seeds but where in the ether
do our souls go
and what do they become.

WHEN THE BLOOD CALLS

Reveille.
My tongue on your...
Your hand on my...
comes the quickening
comes the hardening
comes the rhythmic
urge to die.
Comes the knowing,
comes the driving
comes the flowing
you and I.

BURIED TREASURE

In the hollow of your thighs
lies a treasure like a pearl
lost in reeds of the sea
the tongued duality
not lost to me.
(I can tell honey)
by the way you jump
and by the lidless
stare of your eyes.

SNAPSHOTS - SHORTER POEMS

A DOZEN SHORTS

leaving
the cemetery...
wrong way out

basket of toys
can't bear the sight of them
without her

forgiveness
one word not
in his vocabulary

sea cave
where once we loved,
more sand fills it

bullets through glass
dropped fork
hits the dinner plate

lunar corona ...
we dance around questions
that hang in the air

gift exchange
Valentine's Day
red rose, blue pill

wildfire...
this compulsion she has
for testing limits

not feeling joy...
I borrow the sound
of songbirds

DNA test
am I the man
I think I am

the one
that got away...wasn't
who you think it was

Variation on a Theme by e.e. cummings
(after... "silence .is)

love
.is
a
smiling

girl:the

birth
ing:gold of
sky

gazing before dawn

because
you kept your secrets
and I kept mine
we didn't entwine

ANTICIPATION

Before I see
I smell it,
the sea behind
the mountains.

SPIRITS ELEMENTAL

Always near water
I think of your
earth, your fire
and the air sings.

GIFTS

The Moon said to the River
"I give to you my light,"
and the river replied
"And I to you, my song."

DESERT SOLITUDE

Blessed with stars
this desert sky,
yet I stand alone
beneath them.

NESTING

Alone in the house
all day long the riffle
of turning pages

ANTICIPATION I

Does a woman planting seeds
feel the swelling of earth,
or a man seeing the gun flash
feel the thud before the bullet hits?
Does senility crack the heart
before the mind?

LESSON LEARNED

A much beloved uncle
taught me not to kill,
he made me eat the bird
I'd shot, hot just off the grill.

    My snake tongue
  slithers through your grass
   searching for the yolk
    in a pearl pink egg.

BUTTERFLY

To crawl upon earth;
to sleep cocooned
in dreams of flight,
to awaken shorn
of chrysalis and
don wings, thin
as paper lace,
to fly.

**TRIPTYCH FOR
CANADIAN GEESE**

A squadron of geese.
How many wingbeats,
between the Arctic
and Tierra del Fuego?

Is your honking
for the joy of flight
or just a worker's
cadence?

A lone goose heads South,
a different drummer perhaps?

APPLE RED

the badge of her kiss
worn like a scar on my cheek.
I let the sun flake it,
rain wash it, wind
carry its stamp away.

Why not,
I earned it

LEAVES

Leaves above me
yesterday, today
beneath my feet

Autumn leaves
where will the stream
take them?

TWO ON TWILIGHT

I see the gnats
and then the bats
and then the gnats
no more.

Where sea, sand
and sky converge
a seagull lands

SOLSTICE 2

Rising, sleeping
with it, the day
of longest light

Waking, sleeping
the sound
of falling rain

CORPORATE AMERICA...

is a fat man,
with a stogie
clamped in
bulbous lips.

**TO DRINK OR NOT,
TO DRINK**

Claiming
sobriety,
his breath
a distillery.

ST. PATRICKS DAY

The gist of Dublin,
says that cheek
gives no quarter
in an Irish pub.
So, drink up lout
but watch your
wagging tongue.

THE PASSING

No caroling this year
where your voice was
now only the wind

VERITAS

We breathe, we live
we stop, we die.

ALL IN A NAME

If what we think of
as Earth is Heaven,
what then must Hell
be like?

SIX GRAINS OF SAND

I am a celebration
fireworks bursting
in a sable sky
dissipating smoke
a constellation's
residue

street noise...
what parchment promised,
just scribbles in ink

in the silence
who speaks
Gaia, a guardian
my own mind's
subconscious?

SGOS, continued;

Hill Country Parody

banjos, moonshine
bootleg cigarettes
kissing cousins
rattlesnake shake
ZZ Top beards at
a shotgun wedding

Patagonia

lisp of wind
In the pampas grass
Gauchos sipping
Malbec wine
on the range
at dusk beneath
the Andes

dolphins at play
in the singing surf
that I could be as free
and joyful

ROUND MIDNIGHT

Jazz
a flatulent sax
melody crunching notes
catching a blue mood
smoke

SOUL SHAKIN' DIVA

woman
Rubenesque, lively
dancing barefoot, her
shoes tossed with elan
a Coltrane jammin',
bird gone girl

MANN ALIVE...

Still trillin'
that Philly dog flute
from Baghdad to Bahia,
a silver lipped samba
pushing notes in moonlight
under comin' home stars

Chimes at dawn
a tranquil melody
murmuring through golden mist
hush

the rose
in the lake that
someone tossed,
is this love
abandoned?

ANNIVERSARY

love letter...
in her hand,
on her heart
as she sleeps.

SILENT CONSENT

In seconds, between
the syllables of a look—
your eyes answer
the singular question
posed in mine
with the unmistakable
affirmation of a smile.

He has an answer
for everything,
even the questions
no one would ask.

MORNING GLORY

Sunrise on the windows
of homes on the hill
across the deep, blue bay

changing tide...
between moon and sea
between you and me

between nowhere
and everywhere,
       t   t
       r   r
       a   a
       i   c
       n   k
          s

not again...
the audible CRACK
of my ankle bone

thump,
thump
pounding
pavement
and the
morning's
peace,
pile driver

TANKA

Stars
luminous, sharp
blinking in darkness
warming the indigo sky
Hope

Learning to bend
like a willow in wind,
to flow like water
and wear down stone.

Lily-of-the-Nile
the glaze of her eyes
as she names it
a memory perhaps,
a life lived long ago

ALL IN GOOD TIME

Least heat moon
brilliant stars burning
in a sky of ink, but
I'm not yet ready
for the journey home.

a fresh baguette
red wine and cheese,
she in her summer dress
only the sky bares witness
to the music we make

at fifty-five
my wandering muse
comes home, to sing
to me of places
I have never known

The mirror sends me
a gray message of aging
lines furrowed by years.
But the eyes still speak
a young heart inside.

Steady, yet flowing
your eyes embraced me -
tear filled, yet brave
you first said "I love you",
and left me forever changed.

Across the sound
on opposite shores
two people dreaming
of each other unaware
they're already touching.

same moon
in the same sky
but oceans away
your voice so faint
I can barely hear it

Alone at twenty
she reads his last letter
Time heals all wounds.
Watching her children play
she weeps...no not this one.

Baying in branches
mournful wind an elegy
clouding my eyes
with remembrance of you
whose smile I still miss

incoming tide
diamonds glint
on every wave
what need have I
of more than this?

Blue skies girl
do you carry yet
a memory of me
as I still do, so many
years later of you

serpentine walk
magnolia and sweet gum
Canary Island pines
dappled gifts of shade
under sere blue skies

feather light he treads...
moccasins on mother earth
the smile on his face
born of high mountain air
and no regrets, poet monk

INVISIBLE MAN

I speak
no one listens,
I have become
a ghost
of words.

INDIGO

How else
to describe this day, this mood
red leaves falling
through a tombstone sky
with only crows for company.

BLUE...

berry, bluebird
bluebell, bluebonnet,
blue sea, blue sky
blue mood, dark
as indigo today.

I will be burned
like an old pagan, ashes
cast to wind and waves
I will become fish food but
my soul will swim to the stars

simple gifts...
balsa wood gliders,
bottle rockets
sea salt's scent and
a popsicle tongue

found cassette,
after thirty years
Mom sings again
her joy so obvious
I smile through tears

PASTORALE

A field's tall, green grass
waves towards the house
on the hill, beside which
stands an ancient willow,
branches waving back.

COMING STORM

Hot sun,
a white wail
in a scream
of blue sky.
Thunderheads.

REGRET

There was no pleasure
in the act, but fearing
Hantavirus and feces
in my food, I murdered
the mouse with a trap.

bullets slam bodies
as their school becomes
a slaughterhouse...
I turn my grief to action
I meld my heart with steel

Steel-caged children—
whimpering for mothers
or fathers imprisoned too
for the crime of wanting
what we have forgotten

SEQUENCES OF PLACE – CANADA
Pacific Northwest (British Columbia)

OAK BAY BEACH

Oak Bay beach
hoarding the moon
my eyes and you

cacophony
from the rookery
screeching gulls

boat for sale
pilot gone
from the pilothouse

tasting sea salt
on your tongue
...gulls sweep the sky

toes in sand
cotton touching silk
rising heat

driftwood
how many waves,
how many years

full moon
orchid's shadow
on the blue wall

Vancouver, B.C.

loping into fog
on Grouse Mountain summit,
black bear and cubs

racket at dawn
black bear recycling
the garbage cans

MEXICO

At Chichen Itza--
faces in stone and flesh,
nearly identical

In the same lagoon
where tourists swim, natives
feeding crocodiles

Fiesta over,
in an empty plaza only
moonlight lingers

Small rancheria--
where horses are shod
and kids run barefoot

largest flower*
twice in a lifetime this wonder
*Amorphophallus titanum (cadaverous
flower) 75 kilos, blooms 3 days every 40
years in Veracruz

Europe

HAIBUN-EUROPE

Kapellbruke Spiders

In the city of Luzern, Switzerland stands the Kapellbruke (Chapel Bridge), a wooden bridge with a Water Tower which serves as the symbol of this lovely town. The bridge strides the Reuss River and was built in 1333. For an American, it is incredible to walk on a wooden bridge that predates the European discovery of the Americas by 150 years. Walking on the bridge I thought of all the footsteps that preceded my own. Extending the metaphor further, I thought of the millions of spiders whose webs were spun above me in the beams.

Their generations too had traipsed through 700 years; their lives had been lived, their webs broken to be raised again by their descendants. The moment of this realization was profound for me as it connected dim past, with a dim future whose connection was the moment.

> as long-lived as
> the wooden bridge,
> resident spiders

SKETCHES OF SCOTLAND, ENGLAND AND WALES

For ages
riding Uffington hills
the white horse

Chalice Well,
the cool, clear water
tastes of iron

Stonehenge,
within the circle
only crows may roost

Tor in the mist—
first the whistle
then the falcon

Abbey ruins...
an orange tabby
and my wife's tears

In the stone angel's hands...fresh cut roses

Salisbury's spire,
pointing the way
to heaven

Screeching my eyes
awake, the gulls
of Inverness

Stirling Castle,
the church gargoyles
leering into space

Silently,
the kestrel swoops
...poor mouse

Amidst grazing cattle
and sheep, castles
of long dead kings

English countryside
beside rails of cold steel
everyman's garden

Miles of barley bales,
sipping uisque beath*
from my flask

*Scots Gaelic, "water of life"
whiskey, made from barley)

FRANCE, SWITZERLAND, GERMANY

horseshoe crab...
on another sixth of June
helmets in the sand

palm trees of Ticino*,
how do they bare
the snows of Winter?

*Italian speaking canton in Switzerland

Maulbronn monastery,
she refuses to take
a vow of silence

SPANISH SEQUENCE

In courtyards...many tongues
moon over Andalusia
in field the harvest begun

walls...eggshell thin
in the next room bathing
a woman sighs

rhythmic stamping
flamenco gaiety...ole'
at home...leaves turn

miles and miles
of olives...olives...olives
and vineyards, vineyards

poetry in stone
fragrant Alhambra garden
cats begging food

cicadas buzz
September in Sevilla
cooing doves spin

sun painted palms
glazed in pastel pink
flowers deck the walls

a moveable quilt
clouds conjure shadows
on each hill a tree

Olive tree in Palma,
fourteen centuries old...
and still bearing fruit

African winds
night and day combatants
lightning...screaming birds

GIBRALTAR SEQUENCE

"Born here," she said,
never left the rock
three square miles

Nelson's buttons
in museum's glass case
change in pesetas

fabled Gibraltar
green sea claws granite
screeching apes

in the moonlight
Poseidon's milky dome
emerging from sea

stealing cucumbers
from my wife's had
simian thief

Dover chalk isle
In a Spanish ocean
Albion defiant

EUROPE AND THE ADRIATIC

ITALIA

Napoli—
through an open window
Pavarotti

Byzantine mosaic
the eyes of Jesus
following me

Juliet's statue
bronze burnished gold
a million hands

Portofino night--
thousands of floating lanterns,
sea born Milky Way

On the top
of Pisa's leaning tower
bees and vertigo

The Colosseum, Rome
a tourist screams
echoes

The Amalfi drive--
on a cliff climbing bus...
"Hail Mary, full of grace"

Morning, Venice
sun tags the gondolas
slowly rocking

MEDITERRANEAN/AEGEAN I
(Spain, Italy, Greece)

Barcelona—
strum of guitars,
taste of paella

La Ramblas
the young thief foiled
by a lit cigarette

Roma,
walking in Caesar's footsteps,
I trip on forum stones

Blue Grotto,
songs of the Caprese
echo off the walls

Santorini gulls,
above the caldera
their effortless glide

In silent Delos,
only frogs in cisterns
are heard

Mykonos,
a hungry albatross
feasts on fish

MEDITERRANEAN/AEGEAN II
(France, Monte Carlo, Malta, Greece, Turkey)

Villefranche
where canaries sing
in postcard houses

Monte Carlo
the rattle of coins
in casino slots

Malta
lizards puffing up
in siesta heat

Athens
below the Acropolis
taxi horns blare

swimming naked
in blue/green sea
no one bats an eye

Lindos, Rhodes
the potter's hands
caked by wet clay

Ephesus--
the brothel's location
carved in marble

Blue Mosque, Istanbul
a mullah's chant
fills the air

AEGEAN DEJA VU

Did we meet
you and I,
when these
beautiful ruins
were new?

ADRIATICA
(Italy, Greece, Croatia)

still
can't cross my legs,
eight time zones

Venezia...
church bells scatter
roosting doves

day at sea
nowhere to run to,
too far to swim

Lecce, carved
in the Baroque style
bishops   dragons

Gallipoli...
In azure seas, azure skies
I lose myself

Taverna, Sami
anchovy morsels
for the feral cat

Mt. Olympus...
our 25th Anniversary,
relighting the torch

Dubrovnik...
new tiles, fresh plaster
the war recedes

Diocletian's Split...
in the emperor's footsteps
pagans and priests

Opatija...
art deco hotels, cypress
and pink oleander

Burano...
a rainbow sorbet
of fisherman's homes

JAPAN

KOBE

twenty seconds
years of labor,
lives undone

elastic, that bridge
of concrete and steel,
the best laid plans...

Kobe, Kobe
beneath the rubble
broken dreams

after the quake
yesterday's homeless
joined by today's

a cup of water
a bowl of rice
no rich, no poor

beyond hope
a scratching sound
...sunrise

tolling the bell
for each lost soul
five thousand times

Acknowledgments:
(by title or first line, in order)

Park Visit, White Lotus
Broadway at dusk, Parnassus
fireflies in the wheat field, Frogpond
Sequence - Sojourn South, Parnassus
Florida Sequence I, Mirrors Winter 1993
Edmonds: a Haibun in Four Parts:
Morning Segment: Brevities,
Evening Segment: Moonset
The Day After Christmas, Mirrors, 1997
Winter Storm, Mirrors, 1996
Portland sequence, Bear Creek haiku
Seaview Sequence, Mirrors, Summer 1993
The Rose Garden (Portland, OR), Bear Creek Haiku
New Cicada Kauai Sequence, Mirrors, Winter 1994
Santa Barbara: Rain Sequence, Mirrors, Summer 1992
California/South Dakota segment:
renewal of faith, Drawn to the Light, SCHSG 2015 anthology
Pacific wren, A Hundred Gourds, 5.2 (AU)
Mid-day heat-- Modern Haiku
Morning of the Quake Sequence, Piedmont Literary Review
Terminal, Piedmont Literary Review

Vigil, Spin (NZ),
Drum Circle, Switched-on Gutenberg
The Rift, HWUP
Interlude: ZZZZyne, Raw Nervz earlier version (titled Sex-Ku)
Eros Sequence, Paper Wasp (Australia)
Symbiosis Naturum, Suwannee Poetry
Requiem for a Whale, Peace and Freedom (U.K)
The Tea Drinker, Inksplash, CerBerUS,
Lake Washington, Brevities
Equilibrium, Poetry Explosion Newsletter, Poetry Depth Quarterly
Fleeting, Hummingbird
Unfinished Business, Poetry Unlimited, Suwanee Poetry
Full Time, Hummingbird
Storm on the Cusp of Autumn
Giving Thanks, Hummingbird,
All this…Brevities
Transmigration, Brevities
When the Blood Calls, from
Buried Treasure, Peace and Freedom (U.K.)
Variation on a Theme by e.e. Cummings (after… "silence .is), Midwest Poetry Review
Solitude, Anticipation, Spirits Elemental,
Gifts,
Desert, Nesting, Pastorale, Coming Storm, Anticipation II – Hummingbird

Regrets, San Fernando Poetry Journal
Lesson Learned, Butterfly, Hummingbird
My snake tongue, Brevities
Stars, Hummingbird
Learning to bend, Hummingbird
Six Grains of Sand – VPC, 2017 Anthology
Round Midnight, Soul Shakin' Diva. Mann Alive...Improvijazzation Nation, Raw Nervz (Canada)
Chimes at dawn, Brevities
the rose, in the lake that, Anniversary, Silent Consent, Hummingbird, Brevities, Hummingbird
He has an answer, Brevities
Morning Glory, changing tide...between nowhere
Brevities, Paper Wasp
(Sparrow), Croatia,
The mirror sends me, Steady, yet flowing, Wind Five Folded, AHA Anthology
Alone at twenty, Baying in branches, Kernals, Haiku OR
incoming tide, Blue skies girl, conflicted heart, At the Creekside: (Poetic Reflections)
Lily of the Nile, Haiku Canada Review,
The Right Touch of Sun, Tanka Society of America Members Anthology 2017
serpentine walk SDPA 2017-18

feather light he treads...Kokako (NZ)
Invisible man, I speak, Indigo, Brevities
Blue, Hummingbird
I will be burned, California Quarterly 2018
Across the sound, same moon, Moonset
simple gifts...San Diego Poetry Anthology, 2016-17
at fifty-five, found cassette, Cicadas... Moonset (2). Brevities
low tide, Brevities
a fresh baguette, Hummingbird
bullets slam bodies, Ribbons, Tanka Society of America
Steel-caged children—Ribbons, Fall
Sketches of Scotland, England and Wales, Mirrors
France, Switzerland, Germany, France
Spanish Sequence, Mirrors, Autumn 1991
Gibraltar Sequence Mirrors, Winter 1992
Italia - The Colosseum, Rome, The Amalfi drive

Modern Haiku, Haiku Headlines
Mediterranean /Aegean I,
Mediterranean/ Aegean II,
Ephesus, Mt. Olympus Segments, Frogpond
Adriatica, Frogpond
Aegean Déjà Vu, Hummingbird
Kobe, previously unpublished

Acknowledgment 2:

Scott wishes to express his gratitude to Kath Abela Wilson for creating the back-cover blurb. Kath is a multiple award winner in both tanka and haiku. She won *first place in English language Tanka in the Fujisan Contest, 2017.* Her haiku was honored with third place in The Santoka International Haiku Contest, 2017 "Peace", and honorable mention in the Yuki Teikei Haiku Society Haiku Contest, 2017, and British Haiku Society Contest, 2017. In addition, she is secretary of the Tanka Society of America creator and leader of Poets on Site since 2010, meeting and performing in museums, gardens, and at Salons at her home with Rick Wilson, flautist and collector of flutes of the world. She publishes her free verse, and short form poetry in journals, anthologies and books worldwide. She's author of The Owl Still Asking, Tanka for Troubled Times, and Driftwood Monster, Haiku for Troubled Time, Loco chals, Moria Press, 2017. She has several book forthcoming in 2018 and 2019

REVIEWS OF PREVIOUS BOOKS

Summer's Early Light (1973)
Phoenix (Songs of the Firebird) (1981)
Cascadia and Emerald Rain (1993)
Vermilion Falling (1994)
(Sold Out)

Note: all the limited edition books below may be purchased from the author, as they will not be reprinted once sold out. For further information contact William Scott Galasso via email scottgalasso@yahoo.com.

Silver Salmon Runes, the last book and future work may be purchased via Amazon.com

Haiku/Senryu Collections

Full Moon Serenade (2001)

In Full Moon Serenade William Scott Galasso, the honesty of the poet's perception is evident...the reader hears the poetry speak rather than the poet...there is synesthesia of senses that creates a unified poetic image that enables the reader to hear sunlight and see the river's songs ...unity within diversity...a sense of magic...

A favorite sequence is "In the Beginning";
it is a powerful testament to a love
relationship:

Tasting sea salt
on your tongue
& gulls sweep the sky

Galasso's sense perceptions are vibrating
with song...this book of poetry is a gift to
the reader.

Marjorie Buettner --Modern Haiku

Odori, Blue--2004

This unique collection is well worth the read because it follows Galasso's bold vision. He speaks his truth without compromise, presenting the world to us as it unfolds before him. Where he finds allusive presence, he presents it. Where he finds irony, or pain, desire, or betrayal, he presents that also. His poems are crisp, and honest, written with a deft touch that is uniquely beautiful.

Carrie Anne Thunell—White Lotus/Nisqually Delta Review

Laughing Out Clouds (2007)

There is a sense of yugen (or mystery) in many of these poems. It is a mystery that inspires us to Galasso's poetry.

Marjorie Buettner, book editor, Moonset

I'll never forget reading this collection…the beautiful, insightful and mainly uplifting haiku, senryu and other short verse and mix of prose and poetry resonates with any reader with a soul.

Paul Rance, Editor, Peace and Freedom Press

Sea, Mist and Sitka Spruce (Poems 2007-2009)

Sea, Mist and Sitka Spruce is the 12th book by the very prolific William Scott Galasso...over 150 haiku, senryu, tanka, haibun previously published in a very wide selection of haiku and mainstream journals... I particularly enjoyed the autumn and winter images...

Autumn   Winter

wind gust...   shooting star...
with each leaf fall even the heavens
more sky   seem restless tonight

Moira Richards, Book Editor, Moonset, South Africa

Silver Salmon Runes 2016

This is a large collection of haiku and senryu by William Scott Galasso, organized by the seasons. Reading through the collection, with two or three haiku per page. I get a sense of authenticity and integrity as if I were reading someone's journal. The haiku are well written and accumulate into a sort of autobiography of the seasons. Here is a sampling of two of the seasons: *winter wind/we lean into/each other* and *spring training.../behind the dugout/a new girl-friend*. Galasso includes a haibun, sequences, and senryu such as *sidewalk café'/her love life lousy.../now we all know*.

Randy Brooks -- Frogpond

Silver Salmon Runes 2016

Longtime poet Galasso's latest collection of poems written between 2010-2016. It includes sections for haiku (in seasonal order), senryu, haibun and tanka. While some of the poems are more statement than haiku, Galasso has been writing long enough to provide a bunch of keen observations that do what good haiku do: provide a unique viewpoint on the ordinary world. What is especially enjoyable is the diversity of viewpoints he puts on, covering a variety of ages and situations which makes him hard to pin down. The poems are done a disservice in small type and clustered at the top of a large page. but that aside, an enjoyable volume, *on the inside as it is on the outside rain.*

Marjorie Buettner -- Modern Haiku

If less is truly more, then haiku/senryu is poetry at its best. And Scott Galasso is a master of the form. Within this treasure trove, I plucked a few gems for your pleasure. "sea breeze, the salt inside, answers." ". . . solitude, bitter tea." "home movies, the living and the dead, at play again." A powerful and enchanting glimpse of the world around us and its relationship to our relationships.

Tim Whalen (teacher)

Scott's haiku are perfect. The answer to a busy world.

Peggy Edwards, Author of Alphabeto, Editor of the 2015, 2016, 2017 Village Stories Anthologies.

Available through Amazon.

Non-Haiku (free form)

Rainbow Music (1995)

If you don't plan to buy another small press contribution for the remainder of the year indulge yourself...

Joyce Carbone, Editor, Cerberus

This collection of poetry, encompassing a wide range of subjects and a variety of free-verse styles has been previously published in over 50 poetry journals, magazines and anthologies in the U.S., Canada and New Zealand, including Poets On, Midwest Poetry Review, Bouillabaisse and anthologies, The American Dream and We Speak for Peace.

Paperback Book Swap

Blood (family) and Ink (Poems 1996-2002)

"Galasso utilizes a varied array of free verse styles. Combined with candor, perception and interesting approaches, both simple and complex subjects are made interesting...some real gems."

Martin Latter (Peace and Freedom), Lincolnshire, U.K.

Collage (Selected and New Poems), 2012

Scott Galasso's latest collection is one of the best books of poetry that I have read. He utilizes the poet's best tools of simile, metaphor, alliteration and internal rhyme in free verse style.

His poetry reflects compassion, feeling and contains haunting memories with which we can all identify.

He is a poet in command of his language and at one with the world. He gets us to slow down and look up at the sky, to enjoy the quiet moment, but at the same time he engages us in those issues facing modern man. In their global perspective, these poems identify with the deepest recesses of our own humanity.

In vivid imagery and movement Galasso is fearless in expressing the sublime, the dramatic, the erotic, and the tragic in family life, war, aging, daily living, the homeless, climate change, the seasons, the garden, time and even our currency.

In "DECADES, Part 2" with juxtaposition of films and music with events from the front page, we remember how it was. And the memories of those years continue in the rhythm of the language. Yes, that was how it was and how it is. This is the truth is what we want and don't get elsewhere. this is writing that we trust, a remarkable collection.

J. Glenn Evans, Founder and director of Poetswest, and author of three books of poetry: Window in the Sky, Seattle Poems and Buffalo Tracks. He's a member of both the Washington Poets Association and the Academy of American Poets and is listed in the Who's Who in America and Who's who in the World.

In Collage, Scott Galasso delivers vivid images, colors, and moods in a variety of poetry styles (form and free verse) that capture personal memories, history and the essence of places while sharing beliefs and ideals, making passionate declarations, telling stories and teaching valuable lessons. This collection encompassing some of his best work from 1973 to 2012 is ambitious, humorous, frustrating, compassionate and as honest and nakedly human as anything you're likely to read.

Christopher J. Jarmick, Seattle-based poet and author of The Glass Cocoon and Ignition: Poem Starters, Septolets, Statements and Double Dog Dares (2010)

Note: All photos on location by
William Scott Galasso, except
the photo under Japan, taken at
The Earl Burns Miller Japanese Garden
Cal State University Long Beach
and the back-cover photo by Vicki Galasso
based on a concept by William Scott
Galasso

William Scott Galasso is the author of fourteen books of poetry and the editor/contributing poet of *Eclipse Moon*, (2017), the 20h Anniversary issue of SCHSG.

"I love Scott's leisurely perspective on his life as an adventure. I am so impressed with his thoroughly well thought out viewpoints, sensitive, powerful work, and unusual details. His work is in the spirit of a great journey, literally and literarily."

Kath Abela Wilson, Author of *The Owl Still Asking, Tanka for Troubled Times*, and *Driftwood Monster, Haiku for Troubled Times*, Moria Press.

www.ingramcontent.com/pod-product-compliance
Lightning Source LLC
Chambersburg PA
CBHW061323040426
42444CB00011B/2748